Crosswords

A second collection of poetry

Jennifer Hetherington

First Published: 2023

10 9 8 7 6 5 4 3 2 1

ISBN 978-0-6454326-1-9

Printed in Australia

Published by RoseyRavelston Books

roseyravelstonbooks.com.au

To Family.

As the author, I'm grateful that this work has been inspired by and written in the remarkable lands of the Gumbaynggirr and Ngambaa peoples. I acknowledge our Aboriginal and Torres Strait Islander Peoples as the Traditional Custodians of the Land, Rivers and Sea, and pay respect to the Elders; past, present and emerging of all Nations.

Jennifer Hetherington

Contents

All illustrations by Jennifer Hetherington

Black Magnolia

Do go gently into the hour of daybreak
with footfall affixed, extremities wrapped
in a spreading, enlivening bodily yawn.
Find the tree, the stone, the beach.
Peddle madly against the sand to gain the reach.

Dawn works her celestial charm,
as Mother sun beams love on the leisurely rolling
globe.
Her sigh reverberates in the depths of blue planet
ocean.
Tempted to fall apart, the chain adrift, yet seven
sequences call you in.
The lift, the shout, the rush, the tremors…
undeniable.

Do go gently into the hour of dusk,
though watch out for transportations bent on
sweeping you away.
As the black tulip magnolia blooms, the
dominion of demise is again eluded.

The exit visa is locked elsewhere, immersed in crimson bindings.
No need to pump the sticky peddles so violently,
There's the sign, more languid tracks to travel.

✱✱✱

Lock It

Held her face
Kissed her hair
Caressed the ribbons binding
Links of solid silver
broken only by the glint of sunshine.

Suppress the placid profile
Not with loss of feeling
Was it ten to two am or pm?
The last face held
however drawn or delivered
Effecting relief of dulled eyes registering
grief too soon.

✳✳✳

Big Ben

When least expected, I sometimes realise I've drifted off…
To another place and time. An era that seems so recognisable.
Yet impossible for me to have lived through.

Encountering scenes of 17th century privation,
juxtaposed with extravagant frivolities…
Makes my supposedly lucid head spin.

Not asleep and dreaming, the view is vivid,
colourful, sharp and arresting.
Language and gesture mingle with scents
so rarely detected in 21st century existence.

My skirt hems waft and muddle with Thames River mud
and unmentionable effluent.
A fog of grey precipitation mists the eyes of sullen Londoners,
busy in forbidden yet necessary pursuits.

My awareness yields,

    as Big Ben strikes 5am.

✹✹✹

Robe Manor

The slice on my thumb,
    blady grass.
Blistered toes,
    new gum boots.
Cracked lips and hands,
    grazes from blackberry clearing.
Broken window panes,
    collected, not strewn.
Unbroken hearts and souls,
    Heads in the clouds.
Thundering gales,
    shivering tales.
Power mountain gifts,
    memories to prevail.

✷✷✷

Mother's Day

Some days we wake thankfully
to sunshine or rain.
Other days to a mist of history
  as she would have done.

Sometimes her vital energy was awakened
by familiar voices on the phone.
Detecting unknown speech
  made her cracked and cautious.

Somewhere she is now in endless rest
beyond the flooded ground.
Bodily absent, though shallow buried
  in my heart.

(Dedicated to Myra H- b.1925 d.2020)

✲✲✲

Dragonfly

Ah! I'm not sure that my death has been final. She wonders hither, a tiny human angel. My clinging body, fragile, yet seemingly stable. Oh, hello, aren't you beautiful. A statement ringing in both our juvenile brains.

Though I was resigned to the fact that my short existence had run a natural course, ending in my demise, my three foot tall pixie was determined to be my saviour. She needed me. I looked into her young eyes, and saw the future. Not mine, mine was finite, hers stretched into the next millennium.

Wrapped gently in freshly laundered cotton cloth and carefully ensconced inside a jam jar, we set off on the mini sojourn. This is a life I've never known, but I can hear her breathing, and her footsteps, and the sway of the small case that I am contained in has as well as a lovely strong aroma of mandarin. The hue dances in my dead eyes as I recall the myriad of colours that had radiated from my wings.

I am now unwrapped, open to the landscape. The wide sky stretches larger than I ever knew was possible. We slumber, she reclined at the base of the vast gum tree, me avoiding counting the moments that slip by. A black snake slithers past our prone bodies. She is not disturbed, we are not a threat to her welfare or her family, and we are definitely not the source of nourishment she is seeking.

The cattle roam closer as my tiny angel dreams. Her visions unfold in sequences. Brothers expending raucous energy in the school playground, tall shelves of books asking for attention, blackboard chalk fallen after a rudimentary equation, Queen Elizabeth regally oversees the whole classroom. Jacaranda flowers fall as lilac snow beyond her royal highnesses' view.

The enticing aroma of freshly baked scones, the yapping of cattle dog Nip, and a mothers embrace returned us both to the here and now world, though I distinctly heard the unborn sister moan.

You can go to school next year. This seemed to be an unreliable statement in the four year old's mind and me, the deceased dragonfly, silently agreed.

I knew I would live on, a legacy, in her memory,
she would never forget me.

✳✳✳

Lovers

My younger body quakes, rejoicing in the overflow.
Flying inwardly, a kaleidoscope of pleasure.

My older body quakes, cautious of the rising tide.
Summoning me beyond the shallows, out of my depth.

Then the remembrance that I can swim and float,
The fluidity is both exhilarating, and calming.

I can breathe, giving and receiving.
Our limbs converge to keep us buoyant.

✳✳✳

My Shoulder

I feel you on my shoulder as I write the lines.
The sigh, the head shakes are yours.
The twitches in the right thumb hanging on the
spanner,
are mine.

To tighten, reassure, the rumble of the engine.
I call you silently in my head.
'Give me strength…" pleading,
and from beyond you deliver.
Still there on my shoulder,
my crazy educator of import not impatience.

As my Mothers lover, you and she were both
lost in 1950s ideals.
Yet, we as progeny were not bound to copy, but
learn.
As individuals, from first to last siblings, not
sheep to herd.

✹✹✹

Under the Boardwalk

Both can and should exist,
bicycle riders and pedestrians.
There was no way she would or
should stride this beast in a kaftan,
and it had never been her ambition
to be Lycra clad, helmeted and branded
head to foot.

'The seat's too high…'
Oh, why had she been seduced by
the charming powder blue enamel, the 'classic'
style,
famed badging, reminiscent insignia – the
BOARDWALK,
visions of sun-kissed shoulders and
strengthened thighs?
Or was it the easy ten dollar asking price?

New mirror and bell positioned and secured,
seat lowered with the removal of the back wheel
rack,

everything greased and oiled, brakes checked,
Helmet in hand, the mechanics head cocked.
She had run out of plausible excuses
to resist the terrifying test ride.

She used to be a risk taker.

✳✳✳

Between the Sheets

Catch the breeze
Feel the freedom
Hear the creature
　　　As you slumber in semi-awareness

Wafts of unknown fears
Dance between the sheets
Rumbles …
　　　Stomach or sky outside

Not quite a head spin
Is it thirst
Or is it
　　　Hunger of another kind

Foot twitch, nose scratch
Hair bothering the eyes
How late or early is it
　　　Does it matter

What's next, or what was last
　　　What is lurking from the past

✹✹✹

Olfactory Influencers

Wet socks and undies, left to fester on the bathroom floor nasally echo the sodden dish cloth lying limp in the kitchen sink.

Ignore, delay and engage the toaster to char the multigrain, an effective temporary mask, supported by the brewing arabica coffee.

In the first trimester of her second pregnancy the onset of morning sickness was unfamiliar, seemingly uncontrollable, unexplainable as the family trundles with relative joy into their daily lives. Absurd aromas, historically pleasant, now yo-yo in her un-showing stomach, heckling her psyche.

Yet a comforting glow invades her face as the final peg holds the gentle sway of laundered linen greeted by mid-December sunshine, free from pungent, artificial softener products, purely blessed by UV rays.

Tonight the crisp bliss of fresh bed sheets will envelope her gradually expanding body.

And from the window that evening ambrosial layers of frangipani, jasmine and gardenia linger, awaiting touch or breeze, but will be mingled with and overcome by the onset of rainfall, a petrichloral veil.

Her day continues. With Miss Toddler ensconced in the fetid confines of the lively day-care centre, mother proceeds in guilt ridden convulsions to the scheduled hospital visit, an appointment that induces benign repulsion.

A stench of fear, beyond fight or flight, disinfected beyond recognition by natural human intuition, yet so necessary. She waits, permanent impatience, on the shelf, a bubble, her bundle a shapeless, nameless number. Violently colourful posters unsuccessfully aim to reassure and inform as her air-con affected nose drips and her thoughts drift.

Why had her baby-brain agreed to another

evening meal of steak and kidney stew. More toxic spew! Or the task of preparing a seafood feast for Christmas brunch.

The wafting enticement of chopping garlic, onions, basil… all the culinary delights of their well-cultivated kitchen garden fail, lost to the rotting compost bucket.

With the daylight tasks imperfectly performed, she and foetus quietly, solitarily, share a single forbidden glass of shiraz and the remains of a small jar of kalamata olives. The heavens tenderly opened as they climbed into bed, a delicious location for the nocturnal dreams of inhaling the innocent fragrance of a new-born babe, breast milk and cloth nappies flapping on the line next spring.

***

Clean Sweep

All goes out the open window
In a sparkling flourish of motes
Reflected in morning sunshine
Not freely forgotten

It's not as easy as
Picking up a broom
Or mopping away sorrows

The clean sweep is overrated
And impractical with a cobweb tool
Loaded with memories shared
And discordantly borrowed

✸✸✸

Morning Walk - April 2020

After an hour or so reading a crucial conflict chapter of Elizabeth Gaskells epic novel 'North and South', I walked, driven by a need for open spaces beyond the garden boundaries. And yes, I will admit, a haunting desire to feed my nicotine habit.

With the sun filtering through the thickness of paperbark mangroves warming my bare right shoulder, my posture straitened with every gentle stride taken. Passing, and briefly greeting, unknown townsfolk melts the solid wax in my marrow, a balm to my 'cabin fevered' soul.

The return journey had me laden with a fresh pear, avocado, two litres of apple, mango and banana juice and the guilt inducing fags. Sparkles from the Pacific entice me nearer. A photo taken, an opportunity to give enthusiasm and momentum to a resting, dusty, vacant artwork.

A passing jogger throws a greeting loaded with compliments at my casual styling… white linen harem pants, oversized. Colourful clingy top hoping to restrain my unharnessed breasts. Thonged feet. She, Amazonian, smoothly, sveltely wrapped in pseudo-camo tights, matching bra-top, mask and ultra-white runners. iPhone neatly tucked at hip level.

'Well, thanks.' I reply and extend momentary conversation as her lean body jogs on the spot. 'Is it really necessary to wear Lycra to exercise?'

'For me, yeah! Got this new gear online from TARGET.'

Trundling on in my five foot two self, I pondered the thought that every encounter has potential for prose and inquisitive thought, I am home.

✳✳✳

Outage

What you long for has long left you
What you left you long for
Was it thought through?
A move on… through
A miasma… so be it.
Seems that your fate was sealed
Let all previous panics rest
All the needles for the best.

Leave,
Space,
Leave the page.
Wake with the fire
Beneath your feet.

✳✳✳

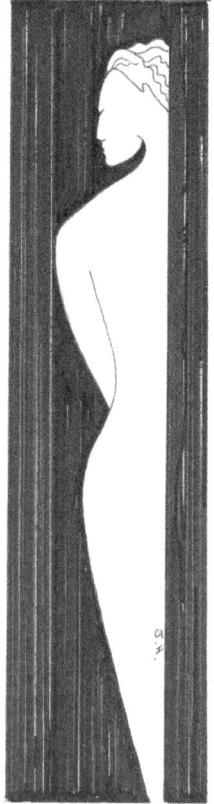

Séance Episode

I'm not your mother or your brother,
or any of your ex-lovers.
But it seems the spirits of them
have inadvertently embodied me.
How do I know so much with limited informing?
How do I instinctively locate objects?
How am I to continue with my after life
while feeling oppressed
by these previous beings?
My appetite for sunlight and pure fidelity
is my only hope of balancing this worthwhile
relationship.

Begone ye ghosts!

✳✳✳

Side-Car

Conversations bounced and reverberated off the vast expanse of service station concrete. Best road tyres. Exhaust system capacities. The functionality and fit of individuals riding attire, yada, yada, yada, as Elic, the Germanic ex-racer maneuvered his black and shiny Yamaha 1200, complete with side-car, alongside the other beasts. Pete gave me a nudge as I eagerly surveyed the three wheel vehicle. 'You would fit nicely in there... ask him for a ride!'

Elic noticed the enthusiastic looks on our faces and proceeded to unhook the side-car cover, wordlessly gesturing for me to make an appraisal of the interior regions. I don't recall the next few minutes, except for the rush of thunderous motorcycle engines igniting. Jacket zipped and gloves in hand I heard Pete say, 'Get some photos....'. I left him pillion-less, but only for a short while.

The side-car seat was low, surprisingly comfy and shielded with a scratchy   windscreen. Bitumen flashed so close in my peripheral vision, vision so exposed head-on. Hydraulics tensioned the trajectory. Two wheelers streamed past, overtaking in time to catch the upcoming cambers. I felt no fear as I fumbled for my phone to make a tiny record of the ride event, and the following morning-tea meeting function.

This particular sort of activity had never been on my 'bucket list' of life achievements, yet my jaw was aching under the strain of a perpetual smile that pervaded my face for those short and enticing 15 kilometres, and for some hours later.

✷✷✷

Pleasant Petrichor

Heaven sent freshness
The song and fragrance dive
But only temporarily
Yet to manifest in later a clime

***

Drains

Rain drains your thoughts,
not entirely.
What was that, a straining of loss?
Sluiced to identify the dross.

Maybe an allusive gift
of affectionate faith and hope
or everlasting nothing?
Drips creating the slippery slope.

A nuisance,
hair that keeps falling
in your eye while writing,
or reading.

***

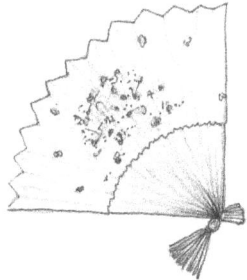

Birdlife

The word was spoken
Then deciphered
For moral profit,
a functional future.

Words went... dissident.
Queries unrationalised,
Undefined. Silence.
Silence the barking dogs.

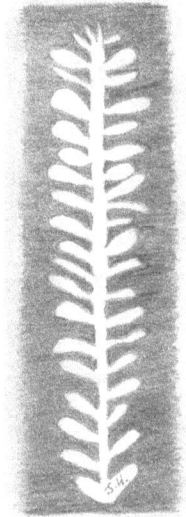

Birdsong is more inclined
In sequence, to tell the tale.
Dawn till dusk.
Knowing seasons and prevails.

Wish me wings
And a new voice
Should I leave my pencil
In the ashes of human existence.

*** ***

Parts

Ears, but doesn't listen?

Mouth, that doesn't speak?

Head, that doesn't think?

Words, that rarely talk?

Feet, that never walk?

Limbs, sometimes broken?

Hearts, ever swollen?

Progeny, ever growing?

Close the photo album.

✸✸✸

Cross Words...

torso, east Texas hills,
in 1876 ways, a head, a man,
a pain, these, love, for a,
woman, hand, to tell, the,
crest, of hair, sure,
Gija, oona, culture,
the sick, each, the use,
canvas, dance, one, tree,
word, is, Joon, stories,
hand, gooy, thrill, year, events,
drown, with, date, told, doo,
scars, as pain.

✸✸✸

Found Books

Meg had finished counting. 'Hmm', she thought, there are 11 books in this sequence, 'one must be missing.' Her mind was foggy, she'd been awake in the early hours of the morning, engrossed in rereading The Time Travelers Wife.

The crescent moon had long since vanished. Birdlife morning chorus was rehearsing. She had drifted off to dreamland with Anais Nin's words revolving in her head.
'And then the day came, when the risk to remain tight in a bud was more painful than the risk it took… to blossom.'

Her contemplations were interrupted as the shop door-bell tinkled. Why is it such a surprise to cordially welcome patrons?

'Good morning. Can I …', she had spun around too rapidly, resulting in the toppling of the books she had just neatly arranged and counted. He didn't loiter, indeed his stride brought him disquietingly close. He was unshaven. His cologne was haunting.

'Ok, let's cut to the chase.' Meg couldn't remember which of them had actually said this. 'Look, there's no need to get the police involved, we have an obvious solution.'

Meg had never considered that the act of rescuing abandoned books might be a criminal offence. She was delighted with how much they complimented the array of other rescued stock.

He struggling to subdue his impatience and his secret, jamming his hands firmly in his corduroy jacket pockets. He squirmed internally, knowing that he must compromise with this infuriatingly formidable female. Her brash calmness was unnerving, and it made her so much more attractive, an opinion that he had been trying to avoid.

'Let me keep the books in the shop, I am prepared to split the profit with you.'

Meg instinctively knew that this gentleman held an intriguing backstory close to his chest. He looked worn and tattered, not a hero, but so beguilingly appealing. Her good friend Maz often reminds her that she has a penchant for attracting unusual characters. Though somewhat perilous, Meg's thinking is that life is more interesting when experienced via a fictitious novel. But this is real. Where the heck is Maz at this odd moment in time?

'Well, alright.' He reluctantly replied, and while offering his hand to shake on the deal, made sure he had the last word, a small victory. 'But I must have access to the volumes, they were my aunts and I have an obligation to list and catalogue them, this could take some time.'

After the hand shake, Boyd turned on his heels and was out the door again as the bell tinkled. Meg realised that her free hand was resting on the spine of one of his aunts precious books. Her curiosity sparked, she relaxed into the newly reupholstered wing back chair, and opened the volume to see a hand written dedication to Boyd, the nephew. 'Dear boy, one day you will understand the value of literature, and my love will endure, Auntie Margaret.'

Think again. Boyd is likely to be another hidden gem.

***

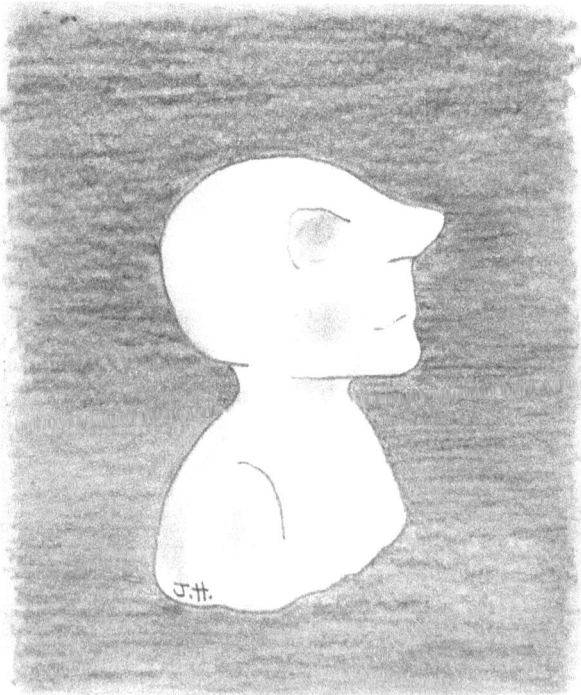

Lemon Spritz

I missed the turn.
Now I'm parked on the road side,
the apron with police tape fluttering
and reflecting the orange pigments of sunset.
Iconic cockatoo calls mock the scene
as they circle and descend beyond,
to splash in the bloated creek.
The old Corona, 1987 wagon model,
hissed in an overheated fuss.
The trusty little bullet seemed now
more like a lemon after our sojourn
of hurtling down the highway.
Like so many before me,
I see the signs of those that also missed the turn,
but did not survive.
Plastic carnations taped to a fence post,
artificial, a false prolonging of regret.
A wooden cross that innocuously defies life, and
death.

✹✹✹

Tip of the Spear

The tip of the spear is-
poisonous, infectious, ineffective,
ill-bent, in-affable, contentious,
vitriolic, unreliable,
unspeakable.

The shaft of the weapon is-
wielded by hands,
that hold no lasting strength,
arms that are not comfortable with holding,
or sharing our familial embrace.

An inherited blame-
mingles malicious moody,
isolated manic intelligence,
lost in notions,
of chronic egomania.

*** *** ***

Loss

She was on her knees,
a moaning nuisance to him,
an itch he'd scratched
that now bored him.
A fantasy unfulfilled,
How was she to know?
His sleeping breathing
fluctuated in dreaming.
One minute frolicking,
next taut, fearful.

✳✳✳

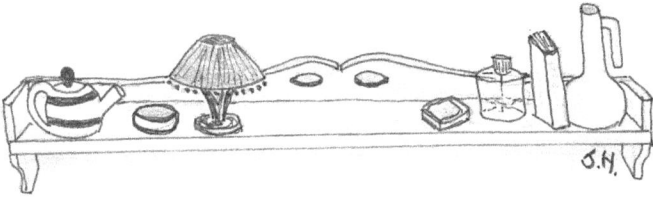

Sprung

Jack lurks in the box, sprung
Ready to surprise and delight
Jack exists for expectant little eyes
His costume will not fade,
as he's doomed to limited light.
Amusement piqued by fleeting fright,
is instigated and deftly assisted
by Mother's sleight of hand.
Eventually she returns the wobbly villain
to the inert shelter of his dim land.

★★★

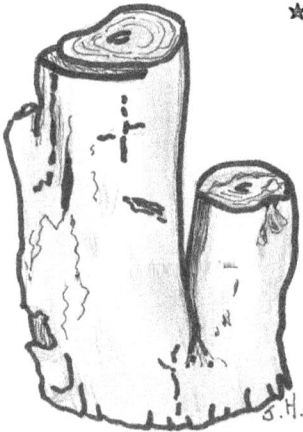

Sunflowers

Today is smiling
yesterday was melancholy
the day before was foggy
      in the early morning.

Tomorrow more grins will endure
regardless of downpours.
For now the bugs and bees
      Are very busy buzzing.

In a few days we will celebrate
and commiserate
the year that was
      and the one to come.
With our universal appreciation
      of the sun and the
          joy of sunflowers.

✸✸✸

Our Forever Summers

Oh Dad! Do we really need to take the old
fridge?
I'd been lumping all manner of stuff onto the
back of the truck all morning.
I'm only ten, what do I know about anything…
that's what my brothers tell me.
Where are they now!
But I like being Dad's helper when the boys are
not around.
So with the persuasive force of 'we-can-do',
(Dad's unique version of Asian skill training),
the Kelvinator and the spare Electrolux vac
are safely secured on the flat bed of the Bedford.
'Keep it front and centre. The flat stuff, like bed
frames and wardrobes will balance the load.'
His logic was perfectly sound.
I stifled my worry that Mum was not so
enthusiastic,
she looked very round and heavy and sighed a
lot.
Making a cup of tea for her in the morning was

nice,

but there was little conversation.

Though she seemed to like my account

of how the chooks were laying.

'Well done girls,' she would say.

Anyhow, this mid-December jaunt was

standard practice

in Dad's busy diary of outings, so we got on

with it.

He never called it camping.

The solitary beach house was a shell,

a tared roof and asbestos walls,

out-door dunny and the luxury of a cold indoor

shower.

Relatively opulent when considering

the tent dwellers in the village, I thought.

After the initial embarrassment of arrival,

hillbilly fashion, we all five of us, made comfort

our way of life.

Not sure about Mum, and the leaky roof

when the wild storms hit.

It was easy being ten, on holidays at the beach.

I wasn't target practice for my brothers

entertainment,

they were older and otherwise engaged, if you know what I mean.

By the third week of January Mum
was really swelling from too much Christmas pudding.

But she still smiled and managed to cook dinners
that didn't involve fish.

...probably because she was carrying a belly full of my twin sisters, a fact proven true in February.

✱✱✱

Tock & Tick

Oh please, not again.
Half-awake in a sea of sweat.
The flying dream again.
How many more cliffs can I leap from?

With one conscious eye
the clock informs, 3.15 am.
Tock and tick measure
Remaining nocturnal hours.

But unreal dreaming continues,
penetrating the darkness,
and my susceptible awareness.
Tendrils real me in.

Secret child is waving,
floating, not floundering.
'My name is Serendipity,
I miss you, can you live with me?'
The shrill alarm sounds.

✹✹✹

Isolation

Gaol minus bars
Isolation with wheels
Comfort without cuddles
Affection with no arms
Toxic thoughts mounting
Sunshine with no shades
Stars with false wishes
Moons with no fullness
Christmas devoid of joy
Roads without exits
Tracks evoking history
Mothering without grandmother
Atavistic traits prevailing
Features lengthened
Fruit moulding
Images flashing
Books gathering
Roasts baking
Birds calling
Practices mellow
Ambivalent self-structured

Structures… doubtful
Weather… confounding
Thoughts… unrelenting.

✳✳✳

Mistaken for a friend

hands held
vague histories shared
trusts unfolded
pitiable, laughable
allegiances of wreckage
betrayal of motives
transcendent forgiveness
denial, Freudian
regrets manifested
vulnerabilities unmasked
disarmed, unprotected
irrational falsehoods exposed
envy, enemies disclosed
unresolved, unreasonable, untenable
anagnorisis apparition

★★★

Shadows

Shadows, I'm sure I've not
                          died.
Shepherds, the herd precariously
                          maintained.
Sanctuaries, or is that being
                          self-imprisoned.
        Pitiless, as nightly detained.
        Clouds, separated, shined.

Observations, the faded flaneur
                          strides.
Gamblers, deftly, slowly
                          poisoned.
Motives, loudly, convincingly
                          defined.
            Awakenings, confused to be.
            Content to be alive.

✳✳✳

In a Fog

A flood of fog
No go zones
Repeated messages
      of imminent failure
Depleted, repeated
      requests for refreshing
not a weather warning
      no Wi-Fi connection.

✳✳✳

Wasps

No power   the first time it happened

No knowledge   of what it was

Body as a game   a toy

A child   no voice

Told the birds   and bees do it

And yes   male cousins do it

At the loss   of her un-blossomed flower.

✻✻✻

Human Objects

Accolades mean a lot
  In a wider world
Gather in community, society
  A different warmth
The smile, the handshake, the hug
   Social curb side banter
   Shared provisions
   Promised cooking
   Needs and thoughts
Walk the dog
  A neighbourly nod
Reclaim and recycle
  Necessary to us
  As humans and objects
Of creation not destruction.

✸✸✸

Mother Rain

Mother rain, drenched in soft relief
Mountain air, misting lungs of metabolism
Muster mud, on weighty gumboots
Master mind, soul and weary body
Mesmerised, by unseen songbirds
Moons embrace, fading yet enduring
Missed no opportunities.

✳✳✳

Moontalk

I talked to the moon tonight

   no words were necessary

Just the glowing light

✳✳✳

Mrs Mac

Beside the freshly cut blooms of summer
sits Mrs Mac, a dear sweet old lady.
Her frail frame contains unlimited love
and patience… and countless cups of tea.
As surrogate grandma to many she commands
great respect.

The vista of flourishing plant life
through the window, reflects her resilience,
yet her strength is betrayed
by the walking stick nearby.

Cloud coloured hair and 'mother of pearl'
complexion compliment her inner beauty.

With memories transformed into age old
photographs and mementos
Her life surrounds her.
The wisdom of the past is obvious,
the excitement of the present is vague,
and the future is unfortunately,
and inevitably short.

***

Faux Fur

Marled grey faux fur inside and out
     hugging inside and out
Hooded comfort
Pocketed protection
Cuffs to muff working hands
Grey to match the days
Till sunshine maintains
     the garden greens
Grey pelt caresses knees
A bear hug reaching for fleecy footwear
Boots that have trodden many soils
     local and far afield
like the faux jacket, they memorised travels
Beyond their makers

✹✹✹

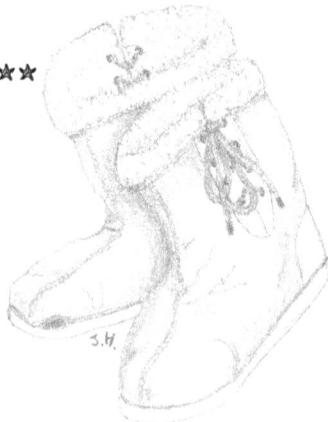

Shifted

lifting, shifting, flouncing, grooving,
pandemic restrictions vaguely looming
damaged, damned, sentenced as a child
to the hollowness of secret shame, internal
blame
sexuality, the problem unable to be explained
shared or adequately named

✳✳✳

Razzey Rovelston

Razzey harboured a secret shame
that of his true name.
No one would care to know it
till the authorities requested he show it.
Was this embarrassment or relief?
With documents in hand
and no acquaintances to give him grief
Razzey acquiesced to the request
and in silence revealed the true Monika.
He had been christened as America.

✹✹✹

Untold

Grieving and loss goes on,
beyond and within lives and deaths.
In dreams and hearts, the soil, and our marrow.

The wilting, shrivelled umbilical cord
of family and humanity.
Suburbanly or rurally maintained.

Not only the Mother, Father, Sister or Brother
        In blood.
Familial still, beyond parental boundaries
        Or conventional normalities.

✱✱✱

The Kettle Boils

the kettle boils
  bubbling clear lava
    settling to infuse
      the desiccated flora
        to cool and refresh
          imbibed from the ancient amphora

***

J.H.

Eastralia

Ah! The band of land

The free

The flowing

The gentle clash of breeze and leaves

Bare feet on cool floor tiles

Wisps of linen brushing ankles

Nodding dandelions alive with bees

A lone rosella wades through grasses

Grazing for nourishment

Swollen clouds roar in a weighty grumble

Rough spikey ice cubes fall

Bouncing on crisp roasted lawns

The maelstrom passes swiftly seaward

Eastralia enters a new summer season

***

About the Author

Jennifer Hetherington is an Australian author, journalist and artist who holds a degree from Griffith University, in Communications (Creative Writing and Screen Studies).

Jen was delighted to have her short story, "In Random's Wake", shortlisted and published in the Lane Cove Literary Awards 2019 Anthology. And more recently, was thrilled to win the 2022 Welsh Poetry Competition with a poem titled "Cross Words", a work that has also been chosen as the title for her second collection of self-illustrated poetry.

Her works reflect, with both text and illustration, the coastal countryside of Northern NSW, the lands of the Bundjalung Nation, where she grew up. After decades involved in the textile industry as a designer, manufacturer and educator, Jen has returned to her love of the creative arts, primarily as a writer of poetry and short stories.

With more collections undergoing the editing process, Jen also has several novellas in various stages of development, all influenced and motivated by the local and emotional landscape that shaped her.

www.jenniferhetherington.com.au